Guidance for Investigators of Spontaneous Cases

Apparitions, Hauntings, Poltergeists and Similar Phenomena

New Edition

STEVEN T. PARSONS

ISBN: 978 1 916427 30 3
Published by Society for Psychical Research
1 Vernon Mews
London
W14 0RL

SOCIETY FOR PSYCHICAL RESEARCH

The purpose of the Society for Psychical Research, which was
founded in 1882, is to examine without prejudice or prepossession
and in a scientific spirit those faculties of man, real or supposed,
which appear to be inexplicable on any generally recognised
hypothesis. In keeping with most scientific bodies, the Society
holds no corporate views. Any opinions expressed in its
publications are, therefore, those of the authors alone. For
over a century the Society has published an impressive body of
evidence for the existence of such faculties and the occurrence of
paranormal phenomena.

INTRODUCTION

These guidance notes are intended to be helpful for those who seek to investigate Ghosts, Apparitions, Hauntings, Poltergeists and related phenomena. These are generally referred to as being spontaneous phenomena as they normally occur without warning, as such they cannot be predicted or prompted.

Since the earliest times, countless witnesses have attested to experiencing apparitions or other ghostly phenomena and thousands of buildings and places have gained a reputation for being haunted. To ignore or dismiss these accounts would be foolish, to acknowledge them as proof without question or study would be equally so.

CONTENTS

Contents

Contents

1 | Investigating Spontaneous Cases

The beginning of every investigation is almost invariably some claim that an individual or perhaps several people have had an experience that they or someone else considers to be paranormal or anomalous. The purpose of the investigation is to discover as much information as possible about the experience and to determine wherever possible the cause of that experience. The role of the investigator is to conduct the investigation using sound methods and good practices and to report the result of their investigation to all of the interested parties.

In the majority of spontaneous cases the investigator will be contacted only after an event or experience has taken place. In other instances, the investigator may become involved whilst the events and experiences are continuing. Although many of the spontaneous cases that are reported ultimately turn out to have an obvious or ordinary explanation, sometimes the investigator may encounter cases in which an explanation for some, or perhaps all, of the experiences is not possible. The point of spontaneous case investigation is to bring some measure of control and measurement to these cases by using established scientific techniques and methods from any relevant scientific discipline.

1.1 *The aims of investigating*

Every investigation should attempt to meet the following aims:

- Establish the nature of the reported phenomena.
- Determine if the phenomena could have some natural cause.
- Determine if the phenomena could be due to fraud.
- When phenomena have no obvious natural cause and no fraud is apparent, then try to learn more about the nature of the phenomena.

Meeting these aims need not be thought of as a stepwise process in which any one aim needs be met before proceeding to the next.

Investigators need to be flexible in their approach and it is more usually the case that the various aims will need to be considered in parallel as the investigation proceeds.

The investigator must avoid the temptation, even when requested, to act as a spiritual counsellor or advisor, neither should they offer or conduct any form of clearance, ritual or exorcism of a location or of any person. These activities have no place within an investigation which is limited only towards undertaking a properly conducted investigation.

1.2 *The nature of spontaneous cases*

It is not uncommon for a case to involve a variety of different experiences, involving either a single person or a group of people. Experiences may be reported as occurring sporadically, continuously or over a period of time.

a. Sensory

Phenomena may apparently be experienced by any of the normal senses, either singly or in combination. Witnesses may report visual phenomena such as the sighting of figures, shadows, fleeting movement, lights or other visual disturbances. They may report auditory experiences; hearing sounds, voices, music or other noises that may be distinct or unclear. Sometimes, they may describe smells, olfactory experiences that can be pleasant and familiar or which may be unpleasant. In other instances, the witness may describe sensations that are tactile; they may be touched or stroked. Occasionally, the reported experience may be more forceful or even violent, for example a sensation of being pushed or being prevented from moving or of being scratched or attacked in some way. Often the percipient will report experiences which contain visual phenomena and auditory phenomena, auditory phenomena and olfactory phenomena or any other combination of sensory inputs, although it is unlikely that an investigator will receive reports of a combination of phenomena that involves the sense of taste.

b. Non-sensory

In other cases, the investigator might receive reports of experiences in which there appears to be no apparent sensory involvement. The witness may only describe changes in their emotional state, experience heightened anxiety, become tearful or a sense that there is someone else close by (a sense of presence).

c. Physical

Witnesses may also report experiences of object movement or displacement, the unexpected opening of doors or the finding of items that have been moved or are out of place. A witness may report small objects being thrown, the sudden appearance or disappearance of objects and in some cases report finding objects that are not ordinarily present within the location. At other times, witnesses may describe the malfunctioning or failure of items of equipment. Usually such reports involve electrical items although it is not unknown for reports to include mechanically operated equipment and apparatus.

The nature of spontaneous cases necessitates that the majority of the investigation process will be conducted under conditions which lack any formal experimental controls. Spontaneous phenomena do not appear on demand in the laboratory. Spontaneous phenomena are just as likely to be reported in a busy modern shopping precinct, a family home or an ancient castle. They are reported by night and by day under almost every imaginable circumstance. Such situations are naturally chaotic and considered by many to be unconducive to accepted methods or techniques of study. Therefore, the investigator must be prepared and able to work in and with such circumstances in order to obtain useful and usable information.

1.3 *Public access investigations*

In addition to those cases in which the investigator has been asked to become involved, there are others in which a location permits access to those who are interested in investigating the location and the phenomena that have been reported to occur therein. Normally a payment is required for such access and locations including historic buildings, tourist attractions and public houses etc. will usually come into this category.

Sometimes the location will advertise its availability and promote the reports of ghostly activity and previous experiences that have taken place there. In other instances, the investigator may approach a prospective location to request that an investigation be permitted. It is likely that the investigator and the location owner might have very different expectations from the visit. Whereas the investigator may be interested in gaining access in order to understand more about the reported events and experiences, the owner of the site will, most likely, be concerned with the financial gain as a fee is usually demanded. Increased publicity for the location is also frequently sought and the investigator must be cautious about becoming the unwitting participant in a publicity drive for the site.

In recent years there has been an increase in the number of commercial companies who offer ghost hunting opportunities to members of the public and several of these companies have been successfully operating for a number of years, servicing a growing interest in ghosts and hauntings. As a result of this increased interest, there is now a tendency by many ghost investigation groups to offer paid access ghost hunts to members of the public. These events attract a diverse group of people, with an equally diverse set of aims, expectations and desires.

With such competing requirements to be met, it is extremely unlikely that any useful information can ever be gained from public access ghost hunts. It is almost impossible to ensure a suitable degree of control over the proceedings and to demonstrate that any tests and measurements have been undertaken under acceptably controlled conditions. These events are at most capable only of producing suggestive evidence. Moreover, the publicity necessary to sell places reduces the little remaining worth of that evidence still further.

Sometimes, it might be worthwhile considering a mutual arrangement between the investigator and the location which can satisfy both parties. For instance, an arrangement might be made which allows the investigators affordable access to a costly location. By organising public access events which generate revenue for the location, this income can then be offset against the full cost of private access for the investigators to conduct their own research. Investigators who make this type of arrangement must consider the implications carefully. However, approached with diligence such arrangements have proved to be useful in a number of cases. The obvious advantage is gaining access to a location of interest which would otherwise be unavailable, the additional time spent at the location and gaining a better degree of familiarity with it may also be advantageous.

2 | Types of Spor
Phenomena

Researchers, including the Society for Psychical Research (SPR), recognise a wide range of alleged phenomena which are referred as being spontaneous. That is, phenomena which are reported as occurring outside of laboratory conditions or not under properly controlled conditions i.e. in the wider human world. These include:

- Pre-cognition and retro-cognition in which knowledge of some future or past event or action is claimed or provided.
- Extrasensory perception (ESP) in which thoughts, emotions or actions of others are perceived. As the name indicates, such perceptions are considered either by the percipient or by others to be outside or beyond the range of the ordinary senses.
- Out of body experience (OBE) in which the percipient experiences leaving their own body and observing some scene or event from a remote viewpoint other than their physical location.
- Near death experience (NDE), similar to the OBE but usually associated with a life threatening situation or circumstance involving the percipient, sometimes when normal signs of life have been absent.

All of the examples mentioned above are commonly reported and the information is often said to have been obtained whilst the percipient was in an altered state of consciousness, for example when asleep or dreaming. All cases involving pre or retro-cognition, extra-sensory, out of body or near death experiences normally rely entirely upon the testimony of the individual and are therefore subjective and any subsequent interpretation of the accuracy of the account becomes a very difficult matter. The investigation of such cases generally only consists of documenting and recording the testimony of the individual claiming to have had such an experience. In some instances, where the testimony may include particular or detailed information such as dates, locations,

c., accurately documenting the testimony and carefully
when the information was obtained and the date that the
ony was received will prove to be helpful. In all cases, the
stigator needs to obtain the fullest and most complete account
the events and the circumstances of the experience, together with
any testimony from third parties which might provide a measure
of corroboration or contradiction. The additional testimony might
also be helpful in establishing if the experience was mentioned
at the material time and in this regard, contemporaneous notes,
records and emails or forms of dated documentary evidence may
prove to be of particular significance.

Whilst reports of pre or retro-cognition, extra-sensory and
out of body experiences are encountered, it is more likely that
investigators will be called upon or wish to examine cases of
spontaneous phenomena that involve apparitions, poltergeists,
ghosts and increasingly, demonic or other alleged non-human
entities. Some of these cases may exhibit components that are not
easy to explain or understand.

i. Apparition

Apparitions are the unexpected and unusual appearance of a
person or object. It is also worth noting that in some instances
no visual appearance is reported. Instead, the witness, by the
involvement of some other sense such as smell or hearing,
presumes the presence of the phantom. Apparitions are reported
in haunting cases but they are also reported in isolation without
any previous encounters being noted. Apparitions may also be
reported as a periodic phenomenon usually associated with
some significant date or location.

A distinct type of apparition, perhaps the commonest which
is reported, has been termed a crisis apparition. There are
numerous examples in which the apparition of some person, who
is usually known but who may also be unknown to the witness,
is seen at or around the time when the person appearing is
undergoing some severe physical or psychological crisis which
may result in or include their death. Crisis apparitions rarely
involve more than a single witness and generally appear in
locations that were familiar to the person, although there are
cases in which the apparition was reported at some distant and
seemingly unconnected location. In such cases it is necessary to
try and obtain some independent evidence relating to the person
who is perceived and also their condition at the time that the

appearance occurred e.g. medical records, death certificate and other witness reports.

ii. Ghost

Ghosts are perhaps the most difficult phenomena to accurately define.

Often the word 'ghost' is used instead of apparition and vice-versa.

For example, the Oxford dictionary defines a ghost as *'An apparition of a dead person which is believed to appear or become manifest to the living, typically as a nebulous image'*. Whilst this definition is broadly in agreement with the majority opinion, there are cases in which the apparition of a living person has appeared and many reports in which the observed apparition was far from nebulous. Witnesses have also described ghostly vehicles, ghostly sounds and ghostly smells and so it becomes clear that the word 'ghost' might best be considered to be a generic, all encompassing word for some sensory experience that we are unable to explain by normal means. In many spontaneous cases the term 'ghost' is also likely to be adopted by the witness when describing a variety of encounters. Therefore, the investigator should take care whenever they speak to a witness or write their report to make it clear which type of phenomenon is being referred to.

iii. Haunting

Hauntings are usually considered to be instances in which the same or similar events are experienced within the same location, on different occasions or by a series of unconnected witnesses. The experiences might be perceived through one or more of the conventional senses. Haunting cases can include apparitions or events that are experienced simultaneously by more than one person. Haunting cases may also have a prolonged history of experiences being recorded. Some instances of hauntings go back decades or longer whilst others have a reputation for being cyclical i.e. occurring on a regular basis most often on a significant date which is common for some reportedly haunted battlefields for example. It is not uncommon for the attribution of being haunted to be connected with an object such as a child's toy or some domestic or personal item. In such instances the item itself appears to be the focus of reported experiences.

iv. Poltergeist

Poltergeist cases are often considered to be those experiences or events that involve physical actions such as the movement or throwing of objects or the forceful interaction with witnesses, for example by being pushed. Electrical and equipment failure or malfunction, the appearance of water, often without obvious cause and the setting of small fires are commonly attributed to a poltergeist manifestation.

Poltergeist cases often may exhibit a pattern of slight, almost unnoticed activity at the start which increases in its extent over time before diminishing and ceasing altogether. Another characteristic of poltergeist cases is that generally they manifest over a relatively short period of time, typically only a few months.

Poltergeist cases have been suggested as being linked to the presence of an adolescent child but there are also cases in which such children are not present. It has also been suggested that poltergeist cases are person-centred as opposed to traditional haunting-type cases which are more usually thought of as being location centred but examples of location centred poltergeists and person centred hauntings are to be found in the records. It is often difficult to separate poltergeist cases and haunting cases as both may contain elements and experiences that are essentially the same. Both types of case may involve the sighting of apparitions, the hearing of unexpected sounds, the movement of objects and events that involve the normal senses either singly or in combination.

v. Non Human etc.

From time to time, investigators may encounter reports in which reported experiences are attributed to some non-human agent or cause. In recent years there has been an increasing number of cases where those involved describe the cause as being evil or demonic. These cases sometimes include reports of individuals being physically attacked, pushed or scratched. Although much less common, there are also cases where those involved attribute their experiences to some benign or even benevolent cause. Attributions in such cases include guardian spirits and angels. Occasionally, investigators may encounter cases in which the cause is attributed to a belief in some form of interface between the living and the dead, commonly described as portals, dimensional or astral gateways.

However, when the reports from this group of cases are examined, there is often little or nothing by way of reported or experienced phenomena that distinguishes any of these supposed non-human cases from any other case except for the attribution by the witness or others who are involved regarding the causal agency.

2.1 *Labelling cases*

There is a tendency for investigators to apply some label or to classify the cases and the phenomena that they are called upon to investigate. There are many sources of information including books or magazines, the internet or social and broadcast media which offer up a wide rage of varying opinions and ideas about different types of phenomena, their classification and suggested causes. Personal belief by the investigator and also by the witness often plays a significant part when deciding into which category a particular case will be assigned. This will frequently result in different labels and classifications being applied to similar experiences, even within the same case; one person's poltergeist is another person's demon and yet another person's altered psychopathology.

Labelling based upon the experienced phenomena or reported events must be approached with care – indeed great care, when it comes to labelling or classifying phenomena in the presence of a witness. Labelling can create false impressions and expectations in those whose experiences or claims are being examined. In some instances, labels may actually be unhelpful to the investigation. The labelling or classification of phenomena and experiences is more likely to result in assumptions being made by all who are involved in the investigation and will affect the way in which the events are reported, investigated and how those events or the results of the investigation are subsequently interpreted.

Regardless of whatever label or system of classification is used by either investigator or witness, the actual process of investigation essentially remains the same i.e. speaking to and documenting the experiences of witnesses, assessing and testing claims that have been made regarding the experiences and then seeking to understand the cause of the experiences. If it is considered necessary to apply some sort of label or classification to any case or experience, then such a step is perhaps best left until the investigation is concluded.

3 | Information

Obtaining information that is pertinent to the case is the primary tool of the investigator. Information may be obtained from a wide variety of sources including, the witness accounts, research, site visits, measurements and recordings, tests and experiments and the observations of the investigator. Throughout any spontaneous case, the investigator will need to be aware of and take account of two categories of information: Subjective and Objective. Sometimes it may not be immediately apparent into which category the information is to be be placed. Nevertheless, the distinction between types of information and their sources is an important consideration for the investigator.

3.1 *Subjective information*

Subjective information is any information that is based upon personal opinion, point of view, interpretation or judgement. Most often, this will be in the form of a report, an account or a description of some experience or event that has taken place. In some instances, the investigator will obtain the information directly from the witness or information may come from archive sources or media reports. When dealing with any subjective information the investigator needs to exercise a degree of caution as it not uncommon for the information to become altered, sometimes in subtle ways. It is unlikely that a witness will knowingly set out to deceive the investigator but there is a natural tendency when describing a personal experience to someone who was not there to choose words or phrases, or to change the emphasis of some parts of an account in order to convey something about the emotional impact of the experience. *"Suddenly, the room became icy cold, it felt like I had just walked into a deep freeze"*. Such a description may provide very little information about any actual temperature change but it does provide a lot of useful information about how the experience was perceived by the witness.

Caution should be exercised whenever the investigator is using information obtained from archive sources and in particular media reports as it becomes increasingly likely that any such account may have been changed or altered. Reporters may change or alter details or they may omit significant information altogether. The style of writing and choice of words may have more to do with selling copy than accurately documenting someone's experience. In examples in which the report or information relates to certain past experiences it also becomes increasingly difficult for the investigator to be able to locate or speak directly to the original witness.

3.2 *Objective information*

Objective information is that which is independent of human experience, opinion or judgement. In the context of an investigation, this usually refers to the measurement and recording of physical variables. Typically, this might include: sound recordings, pictures or video information, temperature measurements or some other form of data obtained using equipment or instrumentation. Objective information is therefore potentially the most useful for the investigator. However, the investigator must be aware that objective information is not always without problem. Errors in reading, recording or reporting data or measurements can occur. It is also possible for objective information to be subject to some form of interpretation and editing, turning it from genuinely objective information into subjective information that appears objective. The investigator should, wherever possible, attempt to obtain the original measurement data or the original visual and audio recordings rather than simply relying upon information that is reported by others.

3.3 *Use all of the information*

Taken as a whole, these two information chains, the subjective and the objective, provide the investigator with the best opportunity of determining and understanding what might have transpired and perhaps discover what is the most likely cause. Sometimes, an investigator who is guided by their own personal beliefs, be those in favour of or against the reality of paranormal phenomena is much less likely to consider all of the information that is available or to demonstrate a strong preference for one type of information over another. For example, a person may report seeing a figure whilst it is standing directly in front of a working camera, yet the camera might show nothing. An investigator who believes only in what can be recorded and measured may decide to disregard and to not document the report from the witness. Likewise, another investigator who strongly believes in the notion that spirits cannot be photographed may choose to document only the claim of the witness and disregard the lack of any supporting evidence from the camera.

In the example given, it is perfectly possible that the witness may have seen or believe that they have seen a figure and at the same time, it is also perfectly possible that the camera failed to capture any evidence of the reported figure. There are numerous reasons why such a scenario could occur but in both instances the investigator has chosen to disregard valuable information which could have led to them towards understanding what actually happened.

4 | Commencing the Investigation

Normally, the first step in the investigation of any reported phenomena will be an account of an experience by some witness together with a description of the circumstances in which it took place. The witness or some other interested party may contact the investigator directly but it is now becoming more commonplace for the investigator to learn of some experience or event via the media or social media. In some instances, the investigator may be contacted by a media representative and asked to participate with or undertake an investigation of the reported experiences.

Sometimes, the investigator may be provided with some form of recording, either audible or visual of an event that is considered to be paranormal or anomalous. Occasionally, the recording itself may be the entire basis for the investigator being contacted, although these cases are comparatively rare and it is likely that whenever some form of recording is presented for consideration that it will be accompanied by an account(s) of some personal experience. Often, the account of the events may be contemporary, in the the form of recent witness testimony or statements. Additional information might come from historical sources, books and archives. Further information may come from secondary sources, for example, a friend, colleague or acquaintance of the witness or via a reporter from the media. Occasionally, the investigator may lack any contemporary accounts and their involvement is sought only on the basis of some historical claim of events or experiences that took place. In such instances, the investigator must rely upon historical sources such as books, archives and sometimes local folklore and gossip for the bulk of their information.

The process of investigating any spontaneous case is generally the same regardless of the type or nature of the events that are reported or how the investigator learns of the case. There are certain steps that must be taken in order to satisfy the requirement for a systematic examination of the case. Throughout the investigation process, the investigator must be mindful of the ethical considerations of dealing closely with people. They must accurately record and document all unusual and unexpected experiences and fulfil the requirement of obtaining and recording good quality measurements that may relate to environmental changes (real or perceived), sounds and images (moving and still). They may need to examine the history and geography of a location. The investigation needs to be conducted in a thorough and detailed manner with each step being fully considered beforehand and reviewed afterwards.

5 | Ethical Considerations

Regardless of whether it is the witness who contacts the investigator seeking assistance or the investigator who approaches the owner or representative of a location that they are interested in investigating, foremost must be the ethical treatment of all those who are involved.

The investigator must ensure at every stage of the investigation that they act honestly, fairly and with integrity, demonstrating proper and due respect for people and property. The needs of the investigator and a desire to carry out any study or experiment as part of their investigation process must never be allowed to take precedent over the needs, wishes and requirements of any person or their property. The investigator must not place any person into a situation with which they are uncomfortable or feel pressured and obliged to go along with. The client or witness should be considered as having 'ownership' and control over the use of every item of information, including all recordings, photographs, documents and other material that relate to the investigation and the investigator must not make use any such material without the prior and written consent of each person involved. The investigator must clearly state how and where they intend to use the material they obtain i.e. for the purposes of their own records or for sharing with other investigators. The investigator must ensure they have prior written permission from all parties involved for any information or material they may wish to provide to the media, use on social media, or in promoting of the investigator or the team. Every individual who is involved in the case must be assured of complete confidentiality and of their anonymity unless they expressly request otherwise. Moreover, they must also be aware of their right to withdraw from the process at any time.

These requirements must be given the highest consideration, prior to, throughout and beyond every investigation.

5.1 *Informed consent*

The principle of informed consent must always be applied when dealing with every witness and any other person involved in the case, this also includes members of the investigation team. Informed consent is the process by which permission to undertake or proceed with every part of the investigation is provided in the full knowledge of the intended actions and of any possible consequences. In order for it to be considered valid, consent must be given voluntarily and the person giving consent must have the capacity to make that decision. Consent must be obtained in writing in the form of an agreement between the investigator and the witness or client.

The investigator should always discuss their intentions with the client and provide information about how the investigation will be carried out; what experiments and tests they may wish to conduct, how many people will be present and when they would wish to visit. The agreement must also include permission for the recording of interviews, the making of maps and plans and the taking of photographs or videos and describe the intended use, storage and dissemination of all such material. The agreement between the investigator and the client must provide the option for the person to cease or suspend the investigation at any time.

The Investigator must avoid obtaining a consent to investigate which contains little or no information or detail. The client's consent for the investigator to carry out *'some experiments'* is not an agreement for the investigator to undertake any test or experiment they wish, especially those which may cause concern or distress to anyone. The investigator must never presume consent has been given for anything other than what has been discussed and agreed beforehand.

5.2 *Witness – age and vulnerability*

From time to time, the investigator will encounter cases which involve children, young people or any individual who may be considered as being vulnerable. This can be for any reason i.e. physical, mental or emotional that means that they are unable to take care of him or herself against significant harm or exploitation. It may not always be immediately apparent that a person is vulnerable in some way but once the investigator becomes aware of, or suspects any degree of vulnerability they must take appropriate steps to ensure the wellbeing of the person. The age or the vulnerability of any witness or other involved person may not on its own be a sufficient reason to prevent a case from being investigated but where it is decided to proceed, then additional care must be exercised by the investigator and all necessary safeguards must be put into place to protect both the client and also the investigator. These safeguards might for example include the use of chaperones or by obtaining the testimony of those individuals in writing or by the use of video and audio links such as Skype or the telephone in situations when face to face interviews are not deemed to be suitable. Every case must be taken on its own merits and the investigator must seek appropriate advice in any situation in which they have additional concerns. The cooperation and involvement of the client when considering and developing appropriate methods for conducting the investigation are also essential.

The investigator must also assess the suitability of those members of the investigation team who are likely to be involved in the investigation. They must also be aware and mindful of their own limitations and capabilities and that of others when considering participation in every case they wish to investigate.

6 | The Witness

The initial contact with a witness or a potential client generally ought to be relaxed and informal but not overly familiar. Depending upon the particular circumstances, the first step may be instigated by either the witness or the investigator and is likely to take the form of a telephone call, email or social media message. It is likely that at this stage neither party will know each other well and for any subsequent outcome to be successful it is important that both parties are prepared to cooperate and work together. This is especially true in instances in which the location is residential.

During the initial conversation it is advisable that the investigator avoids trying to obtain excessive detail relating to any experiences or events. At this stage, it is generally sufficient to gain an overview of what has transpired together with some basic information regarding the nature of the experience and of those who are involved. A more detailed account can be taken at a later time if it is decided to proceed further with the case. In reality, the aim is to begin to establish a rapport with those involved or who might be seeking assistance. Those who live or work at the location are the primary source of information for the investigator as undoubtedly they spend far longer at the location than the investigator. Developing a good relationship with them is not only beneficial but essential in realising a good outcome for any investigation. The investigator should try to ensure that they avoid pre-determining what might have transpired or reaching any decision about the circumstances of claimed experiences at this very early stage. The investigator needs to listen carefully to the witness and consider the testimony as it is provided. It is also important to ascertain why the person has made contact and why they are seeking assistance from the investigator. Additionally, try to find out the expectations and desired outcome of the person or persons involved. Do they wish the phenomena to cease? Or are they simply seeking a better understanding of their circumstances? Some individuals may desire or actively seek out publicity whilst others will wish their experience to remain completely confidential.

The desire by some for publicity is not a new thing but has become more prevalent in recent years.

A desire by a witness or client for the case or the location to become publicised may not in itself prevent the case from being investigated but the investigator must remain vigilant to the possibility that they may well become party, perhaps unwittingly, to this desire.

The investigator must avoid offering any suggestions about what may have transpired, neither should they attempt to diagnose any experiences at this stage. In all conversations with a witness the investigator needs to exercise caution about the words they choose and their response to information that is provided or to questions that are asked. There are many people whose only knowledge of certain types of phenomena might have come from television, film or the media and a poor choice or use of words or labelling of the person's experience might cause alarm or confusion. Furthermore, it may also result in unnecessary or unwarranted actions on their part including in some extreme instances with them leaving the property.

Following the initial conversation, it may be the case that the witness decides that they do not want to proceed any further. Sometimes, it is sufficient for a person just to have someone listen to an account of their experience or they may simply decide that they wish to go no further. This may be frustrating for the investigator but the decision must be accepted without further question and without any attempt by the investigator to persuade them that more action is needed. In most instances, it is acceptable for the investigator to offer some contact information to the person should they wish to seek further assistance in the future. However, it is more likely that the witness will request the investigator to undertake some form of an investigation.

The nature of the investigation can take several forms. These may range from merely documenting experiences and events or carrying out of additional research relating to the location to spending time at the location carrying out substantial measurements and observations. It may not yet be clear which type of investigation is being requested or is required.

At this stage, the investigator must consider if their involvement would be beneficial to the person. For example, it may become apparent that it would be unethical to continue or they may be unable to meet the desired outcome of the person. Investigators are reminded that their primary role is to investigate the claim that some unusual event or experience has taken place and there are a lot of situations in which an investigation simply cannot be conducted due to the particular circumstances that are prevalent. The investigator must avoid any temptation, however strong, to act as an agent for the relief of the client. This is not the role of an investigator and as such is outside of the aims and objectives of conducting the investigation, i.e. to gain an insight and hopefully an understanding of the nature of the experience or events that have been reported. However, it is acknowledged that some instances, relief for a witness or client may well be obtained by the information or a discovery that might be revealed during an investigation.

6.1 *Meeting the witness*

If it has been decided by both the witness and the investigator that the case is to proceed further, then the next step will normally be to arrange a meeting. The initial meeting should be informal and continue with the intention of developing a good relationship with the witness. It is often most helpful for the meeting to take place at the location in which the experiences have occurred but any mutually convenient place will suffice. Particular care needs to be applied in those cases which involve private domestic settings. In these circumstances, the investigator is advised to avoid attending any meeting alone and encourage the witness to have a friend or family member in attendance. When selecting a partner to attend the meeting with them, the investigator needs to consider the age of the witness, their gender, ethnicity and vulnerability – actual or potential. Whilst it is sometimes tempting to include multiple team or group members at the meeting this is to be avoided as it may cause the witness to feel uncomfortable or intimidated.

6.2 *Managing witness expectations*

When meeting a witness or prospective client for the first time the investigator is advised to consider their attire and appearance and of those who are accompanying them. Those experiencing unusual phenomena are drawn from all ages and walks of life, first impressions count.

In instances where the witness has sought out and contacted the investigator requesting their involvement they may already have certain expectations. Sometimes, these expectations may have come about as a result of some ghost hunting television programme they have watched but it is also likely that the person will base their expectations upon the investigator's social media or internet presence. Investigators frequently use their website and social media pages to emphasise the serious intent of the investigator and the site may contain words such as *scientific, professional,* and *expert.* Alternatively, their website or social media pages may describe the beliefs and ideas of the investigator. The investigator needs to be aware that these will create an impression and an expectation for the witness. In rare instances, some witnesses or clients may consider the investigator to be less skilled because they do not act like the television investigators, though it is more likely that they will be less appreciative of an over-zealous investigator who arrives at their home with an enormous quantity of ghost hunting equipment.

Upon arrival, the investigator should not overlook the basic pleasantries and introductions and offer some form of acceptable identification, for example a driving licence rather than your team membership card.

Do not immediately commence with questions about the phenomena or the experiences. The intention is to continue developing a good relationship with the witness and there is no need to immediately begin questioning the witness. It is usually helpful to start with some informal chat allowing the person to guide the conversation, although some informal comments about the weather or some other general topic is worthwhile if a dialogue is slow to develop.

7 | Obtaining Information from a Witness

It is not unusual to find that a witness will begin the conversation by immediately launching into a full description of their experiences, often with a muddled timeline, jumping back and forth between events or experiences that may have taken place over a protracted period of time. In addition, any friend or family member who is also present may prompt the witness or add further information of their own, sometimes relating to their own experiences, ideas and opinions. The investigator can easily become overwhelmed by this torrent of information causing them to miss significant details or to lose track of the events and the timeline.

Sometimes the witness may become reluctant to talk about their experiences or feel foolish describing them to the investigator, constantly seeking reassurance from the investigator during the conversation. At other times, they may become reluctant to discuss their experiences in front of a family member or friend or they may turn to them for additional support and reassurance during the conversation.

If it is considered safe and ethical then in some instances the investigator may suggest that the friend or family member might wish to step into another room nearby so that the witness and the investigator may speak without further distraction. In these situations, the second investigator might be able to talk to the friend or family member and document any information they may have or wish to add. However, if the witness indicates any reluctance to be apart from their companion then this must be respected.

Every witness will be different and likewise, every meeting will be different. The investigator needs to carefully assess each situation and continually adjust their approach according to the prevailing circumstances. Throughout the conversation, the investigator ought to be guided by the witness but needs to avoid being led by the witness or their companion. At this stage the investigator only requires basic information relating to the experience, the events and to ascertain the timeline, as it is not always clear at this stage if an investigation is either needed or is practical to undertake.

It is helpful if the investigator makes some brief notes or whenever possible record the conversation. Recording allows the investigator to focus upon the conversation with the witness without the constant distraction of needing to write notes. However, it is important that the witness fully consents to the conversation being recorded beforehand and that they are either offered a copy of the recording or are encouraged to also record the conversation if they desire. Some investigators may consider video recording the witness interview but it is often better to avoid the use of video recording equipment, particularly, at such an early stage. Many people are uncomfortable in front of a camera and in addition they may become more self aware, concerned about their appearance perhaps or how they are being perceived. A video camera normally requires some setting up, together with any lights and tripods etc., which is not only distracting but also time consuming. Audio recording is much simpler to undertake, is less intrusive and is therefore less stressful for the witness and often for the investigator too. It is almost always the case that when the witness feels at ease, they will normally be forthcoming describing and talking about their experiences or the events that have taken place.

7.1 *Be guided and be clear*

Often, a witness will express strong opinions about the nature of their experiences and what they represent, the reasons and the causes. The investigator should listen to and accept what the witness is saying and use that to guide their responses but the investigator needs to avoid it becoming a situation in which the witness demands an explanation for their experiences and in particular avoid any confirmation that an experience is paranormal. The investigator needs to maintain an impartial and non-judgemental attitude regardless of their own opinions, ideas or beliefs. The investigator must take care not to offer or suggest an opinion or attempt to diagnose or explain the experience of the witness at this early stage.

If the client is seeking an outcome that involves the cessation or resolution of the events, then the investigator must make it clear that the role of an investigator and the purposes of an investigation is to seek wherever possible an understanding and in some cases an explanation as to the nature of the experience or the events. Whilst it is not the task of an investigator to put an end to these experiences or events it is often the case that an understanding or explanation gained as a result of the investigation process is sufficient to cause any further experiences to either cease entirely or to diminish to a manageable degree. If it becomes clear that the witness is requesting the investigator to conduct some form of ritual or exorcism, then the investigator must politely decline any further involvement if they are unable to persuade the witness from this course.

7.2 *Beginning to understand*

Following this initial meeting and conversation, if it has been agreed that an investigation will be undertaken, the investigator needs to begin the process of trying to understand the witness's experience and the claims that are being made. At this stage, the investigator may find that it is helpful in most instances to ask each witness to write down in their own words a description of their experiences. The witness should be encouraged to include the dates and times and as much detail about the experiences or events as can be recalled, even if the witness considers it is trivial, silly or unlikely to be of interest to the investigator. It is worthwhile to also request that the statement be written without the witness consulting with, or speaking to, anyone else involved in the case. In most instances, the witness will require some time to consider and write down the information and describe their experiences. The investigator may offer to return to collect the statement after a suitable period of time, perhaps a few days. In rare instances, the witness may be reluctant or unable to provide a written statement in which case it is acceptable for the investigator to elicit the information from direct questioning. Once a statement has been obtained, the investigator should read it thoroughly and acquaint themselves with the key information it contains.

Once the investigator has reviewed the information, then he or she can arrange to re-visit the witness and carry out a further interview.

7.3 *Keeping an investigation diary*

At this stage it is common for investigators to request that the witness commence the keeping of a diary of their experiences. This can be a helpful step that provides the investigator with information about any continuing experiences and offer the investigator an insight regarding the nature of experiences. The diary should include basic information about who had the experience, where it occurred, when it occurred and a description of what was experienced. An additional diary also needs to be commenced and maintained throughout the investigation by the investigator and others in the investigation team, recording their own experiences, or lack of, together with any other salient information they may wish to include.

Many people will have access to audio recording, photography or video in the form of a smart phone or tablet computer. In these instances, it may be worthwhile asking the diarist to make recordings of anything they might experience. Generally, they are often close to hand and can be quickly used and may provide the investigator with additional information.

Although a diary can be a valuable source of information, the investigator must also be aware that keeping a diary is likely to affect the way in which an individual perceives subsequent events and experiences. Requesting that a diary be kept can result in people attributing a greater significance to experiences than might previously have been the case. Events that ordinarily might have been ignored or considered as being mundane or irrelevant may now become noteworthy. Family members or work colleagues may also become aware of the diary and in some instances may themselves be asked to note down their own experiences. People with previously no interest in the events, or who had never considered events to be in any way significant, may begin to make attributions of an unusual or even a paranormal cause for those events. Due to the heightened awareness, commencing and maintaining a diary often can result in an increased number of unusual experiences that are noted and the investigator needs to be aware of this likelihood. In rare instances, this can result in the witness blaming the investigator or the process of investigation for causing the number of experiences to increase.

8 | Interviewing Witnesses

Accurately documenting each interview is important and ensures that no important information is missed or overlooked. Some investigators may prefer to work through a list of prepared questions, some may use some type of questionnaire. Either method is acceptable but the investigator should avoid the interview becoming a tick-box exercise in which questions are asked just because they are written on the paperwork. Having some questions prepared in advance is helpful. It is sometimes easy to fail to ask important questions, sometimes regarding the most basic details when dealing with a witness who is keen to share their experiences in a jumbled torrent of information and mixed up details and timelines. Throughout the interview process the investigator must treat the person with courtesy and consideration at all times and treat their property and belongings with due respect.

8.1 *Ask the right questions*

Before commencing any interview, the investigator must ensure that the witness or person understands that they do not need to answer any question(s) and that they do not have to provide a reason for that decision.

Moreover, the investigator should not pursue any question which the person has stated an intention not to answer. The manner and wording of questions and the way they are asked can have a large bearing on the outcome of any interview and the value of the information that is obtained. The investigator should always avoid asking leading questions such as, 'Whereabouts did you see the ghost?' Instead the questioning may be phrased in a more neutral way that will illicit much the same information, for example, 'Can you tell me about your experience?'

There are established methods that the investigator may usefully employ to help the witness recall and provide information. The interview needs to be conducted in a non-distracting environment that allows the witness to focus solely upon answering the questions and recalling information without competing distractions. Attempting to carry out the interview whilst the witness is actively caring for children or carrying out some domestic task should be avoided whenever possible. If such circumstances continue or prevail it may be better to rearrange the interview for a more suitable time or day. The witness should be interviewed on their own unless they specifically request the inclusion of another person. In these circumstances the investigator should agree but request the companion to remain passive and also that the witness does not consult their companion. The witness can often be encouraged to recall events is by asking them to recreate the context in which their experience took place. This might take the form of visiting the specific location in which an event occurred, the use of photographs and plans or by simply asking the witness to recreate the scene in their minds-eye. In some instances, this might be extended into a walk-around of the location or key areas within it whilst undertaking the interview. This technique has the additional benefit that the investigator can also see for themselves precisely where events or experiences took place and allows them to more fully assess the testimony as it is provided.

8.2 *Obtaining more information*

If it has not been provided in the written statement or if it is unclear, then the investigator should try and obtain as much detail and information as possible about:

- Times and dates which the experience/s took place and the duration of events.
- The chronology of the experiences and of events. Establish a timeline so far as possible
- The location of the witness for each separate experience, their position, viewpoint, if they were seated, standing or moving about.
- Information about what the witness was doing beforehand.
- What the witness's state of mind was beforehand?
- What the witness did during the experience or event and immediately following its cessation.
- Who else was in the location at the time of the experience and where they were situated? Did they too witness anything or not?

- Has the witness informed anyone else about their experience or the events?
- The physical circumstances at the time of the experience, the lighting, temperature, what else was taking place?

8.3 *Multiple witnesses*

In many cases there will often be additional people involved. These may be neighbours, friends or relatives of the primary witness. These individuals may have had experiences of their own that might corroborate or sometimes contradict the primary witness's account and each will need to be dealt with separately. Some people may not wish to assist the investigator or participate in the investigation or in rare instances it may be that the primary witness does not want them to be consulted or become involved. The wishes of all persons must be given priority over any desire on the part of the investigator to consult or question anyone. However, it will generally be the case that most people will readily offer their support and assistance. Each additional person should be interviewed in the same manner as the first witness and their account thoroughly documented.

It is important that every possible source of potential information is considered not only from those who claim to have had an experience or have knowledge of the circumstances. It is frequently the case that others who live, work or visit may have never had any experiences or witnessed anything untoward. This information should not be overlooked as information that relates to non-experiences is just as important as recording the testimony of those who claim to have experienced something. Occasionally, the investigator may encounter or become aware of a potential witness who will, when asked, deny having any knowledge of the events – they may even be dismissive of the experiences of others that took place in their presence. In these circumstances the investigator should document the person's comments and avoid pressing them to provide any further information. In some cases, the person may decide to reveal more information or describe experiences of their own at a later time.

When conducting any interview, it is important that the investigator properly documents the testimony of the witness however unlikely or strange it may seem. In the majority of instances, the person will be providing a truthful account of their personal experience. At this stage the investigator should avoid questioning the integrity of the witness directly.

Immediately challenging the witness, suggesting that they were mistaken or even fabricating their account is a sure and certain way to destroy the investigator / witness relationship that is necessary for the investigation to proceed.

8.4 *Asking questions – sensitive matters*

Many investigators routinely include questions that are of a personal or sensitive nature. Questions about the mental health of a person or of family members, information about medication, drug or alcohol use and even sexual orientation are frequently included in questionnaires used by many investigators. Such questions are not only highly intrusive but in the majority of cases they are unnecessary in terms of carrying out an effective investigation and should not form a routine part of any witness interview.

Furthermore, it is meaningless to ask any such questions without the necessary expertise to understand the responses. For example, a proper understanding of how a particular medication might affect a witness is not something that can be gained just by using the internet or other information source to look up the side effects of the drug and then relating those to the witness and their experience. This approach will only lead to assumptions being made by the investigator that are at best misleading. Questioning the mental health or well-being of a witness or their family should not be undertaken by the investigator except in exceptional circumstances and where they have the necessary training and expertise to fully understand the answer and to respond accordingly.

There may be some limited instances when it might be relevant to consider asking questions of a sensitive or personal nature. If the investigator decides this course is necessary, then they must first ensure that the person is aware that they do not have to answer any of the questions and are provided with an assurance of complete confidentiality. If the person consents to the questions being asked, then they should be put in a straightforward and matter of fact manner. For example, "*Are you taking any medication prescribed by your Doctor?*" and "*What is that medication prescribed for?*". The investigator should avoid commenting upon the medication or speculating with the person how it may be affecting their experiences.

Questions that relate to mental health or substance abuse should also be clearly put and the answers noted. For example, "*Do you take any other drugs or medicines that are not prescribed for you or which cannot be obtained over the counter?"* and *"Have you been diagnosed or treated for any condition that relates to your mental health?"* Here to, the investigator should avoid commenting upon or discussing the answers at this stage.

In some instances, it may be helpful for the investigator to seek the consent of the witness to contact their G.P., other relevant medical professional or health care provider for their advice and opinion.

8.5 *Asking questions – children and vulnerable adults*

Cases that involve children and vulnerable persons will sometimes occur and these cases pose further considerations for the investigator. It is often the case that a child or vulnerable person may have witnessed some event, have had some experience or may have been present during another person's experience and can therefore offer some additional information or testimony.

In these cases, some investigators may decide not to proceed with the investigation, and in some instances this is the best course of action. However, the presence of a child or some other vulnerable person should not be the sole reason to prevent an investigation from taking place. However, if the investigator decides to continue then they must ensure that appropriate steps and safeguards are used to protect both the witness and also the investigator. These steps must include:

- Ensuring that the witness is accompanied at all times during any interviews or questioning by an appropriate person who should be the parent, guardian or properly appointed representative.
- The investigator should not attend the location on their own or spend any time alone with the witness.
- That questions and conversations should relate only to the events or the experiences of the witness and avoid any discussion that relates to health or mental health of the witness.
- The investigator should not act as a counsellor or advocate for the witness and should not offer to carry out any practise or techniques that may be interpreted as other than information gathering.
- The investigator should be aware of their own limitations in terms of experience, knowledge or capabilities and should

withdraw from the investigation at any time if they feel they have exceeded their abilities.
- The witness must be able to fully consent to participating in the investigation process and be able to withdraw at any time.

9 | Further Considerations

Following the initial meeting, time needs to be taken for a full and proper consideration of the information that has been obtained from the conversation, initial questioning, written statements and possibly a diary. Occasionally, it may be decided by either party that the investigator cannot meet the expectations or the outcome that is desired by the witness in which case it is wiser to withdraw and state honestly that they are unable to proceed. This period of consideration should also be extended to the witness; they may wish to amend the terms of their involvement or even withdraw from the proposed investigation altogether. Once all parties agree that an active investigation is deemed appropriate it can proceed. The client must be informed prior to every stage of the process and be given the opportunity to remove their consent or amend the terms of the investigation at any time.

No two cases will be identical. Whilst there may be common features and similar experiences the details of the reported experiences in each case will differ, as will the perception and the response of witnesses.

Some individuals may be scared, whilst others will be accepting and nonplussed and there may even be some who appear nonplussed but in reality may have deep concerns. The expectations and desired outcome of the investigation will also be different case to case. Some people will seek to have the events and experiences stopped whilst others are happy for them to continue. It is the function of the investigator to adapt the investigation methods and approaches to the particular case and to the people involved.

As the investigation proceeds the investigator should seek out additional information from other sources. It may be worthwhile examining the history of the location, the geography and in some instances the geology of the location. In most instances, the investigator will wish to spend additional time at the location. It is usual to undertake these steps in a parallel fashion. Seeking additional information and conducting research away from the location whilst also conducting site visits is usually the best use of the investigator's time and resources.

9.1 *Spending time at the location*

An investigation usually requires the investigator to spend time at the location. This has some obvious advantages:

- There is a possibility that the investigator may witness the phenomena for themselves.
- It allows the investigator to become familiar with the location.
- It enables the investigator to make or obtain additional measurements or recordings.

In most instances the client will be spending a great deal more time at the location than the investigator and their on-going testimony and reports need to be fully considered and integrated into the overall investigation. It is worthwhile encouraging the occupants to make additional observations and recordings and to provide information on those occasions when the investigator is not present.

There are also potential disadvantages to spending time at the location which must also be considered:

- It is often disruptive to the occupants.
- The presence of the investigators may alter the nature or extent of the experiences that are reported by the witness.
- It may adversely affect some of the occupants, particularly those who may vulnerable or when there are children present.
- It may be disruptive and time-consuming for the investigators.

Therefore, in every case, the investigator needs to carefully consider not only the views and opinion of the client but they must also consider if spending time at the location will serve to provide a greater understanding of what has transpired. In some instances, the reported experiences may be so intermittent that it would potentially need very many visits in order to have any hope of gaining more information than can be obtained from the witness testimony.

9.2 *When to investigate*

With regard to the scheduling of times and periods for any site visit, the first consideration must always be for those who may live or work at the location. The investigator should aim to keep the disruptive effect of their presence and of any equipment they use to a minimum. At all times the investigator must ensure that everyone involved is fully aware and have consented to the presence of the investigation.

An important consideration is, whenever possible to try and schedule on-site visits to those times and periods that coincide with the experiences of witnesses. If an event or experience took place by day, then the value of the investigator visiting at night is questionable. Likewise, if the witness reports that certain people or a particular set of circumstances were present during an event or experience then the investigator should seek to visit when those or similar circumstances are most likely to prevail. This approach may also be extended whenever possible to seasonal accounts too.

Events reported during the winter are best investigated in the winter in preference to the summer months when many of the prevailing physical characteristics such as the weather, temperature, the use of heating or air conditioning and lighting will be significantly different.

Wherever possible, the investigator should strive to conduct their visits under conditions that are as close as possible to those that prevailed at the time of the reported experience(s). Being present under similar prevailing conditions may permit the investigator to gain a greater insight into the reported experience. This can be extended to include all those occupants who were present at the time, regardless of whether they themselves reported any experiences. Likewise, if the location was busy and perhaps noisy when the experience occurred then the investigator should try to attend under similar circumstances.

9.3 *Poltergeists – A Special Exception*

Active poltergeist cases may represent an exceptional set of circumstances to the investigator due to their normally short duration. Therefore, in those cases where the investigator suspects that an active poltergeist may be likely and in which there are continuing reports of activity taking place then earliest possible use of independent recording equipment and additional observers may be helpful. Whilst the ethical considerations must be foremost in the mind of the investigator, it is likely that any delay in commencing the on-site investigation will increase the likelihood of the reported events diminishing or ceasing altogether and the investigator being left only with accounts of witnesses or the occasional video or audio recording to examine.

10 | Planning an Investigation Visit

Wherever possible, the investigator should always avoid conducting site visits on their own. The investigator might be part of a team or group whilst others may need to call upon additional observers to assist them. Before commencing the site visit a plan should be drawn up. The plan ought to take account of the type of location, the availability of access, the nature and extent of the reported phenomena and include assigning specific tasks to members of the group. It is advisable that the plan is flexible and adaptable to permit the investigators to respond more readily to any unforeseen situations.

When considering the number of observers to be used, it is generally better not to oversaturate a location with many observers as this makes the task of managing them time consuming. It is also more likely that a larger group will interfere with one another and cause an increased amount of noise and movement. In larger locations the investigator should seek to obtain permission for several visits and use these visits to examine specific parts of the location in turn, rather than trying to investigate the entire site at once. This has the advantage of being able to use the resources in a more efficient manner and it also reduces the number of people needed.

Investigators should time their visits to coincide with any known times of previous witness experiences or reported events. For example, if a witness has reported seeing an apparition walking across the room whilst they watched the early evening News, there is little to be gained by arriving late in the evening and remaining overnight. Likewise, in cases where the witnesses report events that only occur in the morning, then that is the time of day that the site visit should also take place.

10.1 *What is needed*

Each member of the investigation group should have some basic items, both for their personal comfort and also for the purposes of conducting the investigation. Some items may vary, depending upon the type of location, the time of day and other prevailing circumstances but there are some items that are considered to be essential:

- Notepad, Pens and Pencils. Each observer should keep independent notes and records of any experiences they may have, together with a general record of their time within the location.
- Wristwatch. Many people nowadays prefer to use a phone or device for obtaining the time but in some instances it may be necessary to turn these devices off, making a watch an essential item.
- Appropriate clothing and footwear. The specific items will vary depending upon the location, the season and the time of day.
- A torch, preferably that has the capability to be dimmed. Inevitably, there are occasions when the investigator will need to visit a site after dark or the site may lack suitable lighting in some places.
- It is advisable that whenever possible each observer should also have some additional items with them. Although not essential, they will permit the observers to obtain the maximum amount of information from the investigation. These items include:
- A two-way radio. This allows more effective communication between members of the investigation group. Even in smaller locations this is a useful asset removing the need for observers to call out to one another.
- A camera. This may be either a video or still camera and can be used by the observer to capture additional information about events or experiences that might take place.
- An audio recorder. As with the camera, allows the observer to capture additional information and can also be used to make audio notes in situations where note writing is more difficult. In many instances the use of a smart phone or tablet can be used as a ready substitute for either the camera or audio recorder.
- Food and other refreshments, if permitted by the location. Sometimes it may be necessary for breaks to be taken off site or in a designated area.

The investigation group should nominate a person to coordinate their activities and to liaise with the client throughout their visit. The coordinator must ensure that individual members of the group are aware of any specific requirements of the client and are aware of any safety or other issues that may arise during the investigation. Escape routes and assembly points need to be notified in the event that it becomes necessary to evacuate the location.

The well being and safety of group members are a primary consideration and at all times, the coordinator must be aware of the position of every person in the investigation group and also be aware of other occupants and where they are located.

10.2 *Informing the group*

In most locations, it is helpful for the investigation group to agree beforehand some system for referring to individual rooms or areas within the location. Every member of the investigation group should be aware of and use this system in order to minimise any confusion as to the whereabouts of any person or item of equipment. It is also beneficial to provide a plan of then location with the individual rooms and areas labelled. Some locations may already have a plan that the investigator may be allowed to copy or a basic plan can be drawn up ahead of the planned visit.

Generally, it is preferable for the group members to be provided with some basic details of the case. For example, if the reported experiences are predominantly audible or visual etc., together with some general information regarding the whereabouts of events and experiences. The provision of this basic information permits the group to direct their attentions and any equipment towards places of most interest. The investigator should avoid providing excessive information as this may serve to heighten their expectations or bias any experiences they may have. Some investigators may prefer to provide no information to the investigation group regarding prior experiences or events with an aim of obtaining accounts that are free from any prior knowledge and expectation bias. However, it should be recognised that placing someone into a room and aiming a camera or setting up a thermometer will alert them to areas of interest and types of phenomena that are being examined.

Except for private homes and some commercial premises, it is often inevitable that group members will already know something about the location and this is especially the case for locations that are historic or in some way significant. Often, a location may already have a reputation for being haunted or be host to claims of paranormal encounters as a result of local accounts and gossip or by way of publicised accounts within the media.

10.3 *Team deployment*

Throughout the visit it is better that group members remain in pairs with both partners in close proximity to one another. Any phenomena that might take place will have greater credibility if it is observed by more than person. Remaining in pairs also provides additional safety in unfamiliar environments and acts as a basic measure against fraud. Pairs of investigators should be placed into areas of interest and it is important that they remain in their allotted places and that they refrain from wandering. In some instances, it may be desirable that the same pair of investigators remain in-situ for the entire investigation visit, allowing them to gain a greater familiarity with the particular place they are located and to obtain a continuity of experience therein. This method may also be helpful in revealing periodic events which may occur regularly but have a long interval between repetitions.

At other times, it may be worthwhile changing pairs of investigators around periodically in order to compare experiences. Often, the nature of a location or the environment within, may dictate the length of time group members can remain in one place.

In those circumstances when it is necessary for the investigation to be conducted late into the night then it is likely that some participants will experience extreme drowsiness or may even fall asleep. Either will result in the person ceasing to be an effective witness to any events that may occur. Extreme drowsiness frequently results in an altered state of consciousness in which there is an increased risk of hallucinations that can affect any of the normal senses. Sleep and near sleep can also risk the person entering a dream or near dream state in which it becomes impossible for them to know what is real and what is being imagined.

Similar altered mental states can also be caused by subjecting people to periods of darkness or semi-darkness yet it is still common practice for investigators to routinely turn off any available lighting. Moreover, having little or no light adversely affects the ability of people to discern detail and affects depth perception. It also increases the chances that they will become disorientated, all of which reduce their effectiveness as a witness. Therefore, unless an event or a witness experience occurred in conditions of darkness or semi-darkness, turning off the lights will only have an adverse affect on the quality of the investigation.

Investigators should take precautions against becoming bored or restless. It is unreasonable for people to be expected to remain in one place for an extended period, silently observing their surroundings. Unless the circumstances of the reported events or experiences indicate a strong interest in audible phenomena then participants can be allowed to talk quietly to their partner in order to reduce the effects of boredom. However, it is recommended that these conversations are confined to matters unrelated to the case or the location. In those situations, in which it is necessary to remain silent then the participants may be permitted to read a book or perhaps do a crossword. Quietly standing and stretching or bending can also provide some simple relief from extended periods spent sitting.

Allowing individuals or groups of people to walk around the location is to be discouraged. Wandering around the location, pausing here or there in the hope of witnessing something or chancing upon an apparition in reality is unlikely to produce anything that will benefit the investigation. The method will also produce additional noise and movement that is unnecessary and disruptive. When planning the investigation visit some thought must be given to the provision of suitable breaks for toilet and refreshments or to obtain relief from uncomfortable situations. The necessity for people to move around periodically without causing undue interference to others or to any measurements that are being made also needs to be considered.

It may sometimes be the case that some members of the investigation team will need to take medication and the coordinator should be aware of this requirement and make suitable arrangements in consultation with the individual.

11 | Keeping Notes and Records

Throughout the site investigation it is desirable that each person keeps a record of their own activities and experiences. The notes do not necessarily need to be extensive but they should be updated regularly and aim to provide all of the essential items of information including;

- Stating the time that each separate entry was made.
- It is suggested that a 'master clock' should be nominated. In practice, this may be any agreed wristwatch or clock that has the capability to display seconds. All devices and timepieces should then be set to as closely as possible to this master clock. It is recommended that an accuracy of not more than plus or minus five seconds from the master clock is used.
- An indication of the person's location. When recording their location, the person must make their whereabouts as clear as possible; For instance, stating their position as "On the stairs" gives no information as to where on the stairs they were situated or in some instances which staircase they were situated upon. It is often helpful to include a sketch or diagram to illustrate the person's location.
- What transpired. A concise account of the event or experience together with a short description of the circumstances including before, during and following the event or experience.
- An indication of the location or whereabouts of the event.
- The cause, only if it is known or it is immediately apparent. When an event or experience has no immediately apparent cause, the notes should refrain from speculation.
- The duration of any event or experience.

The notes might also include additional information that may be helpful, for instance;

- Something about the state of mind of the individual, for example, if they were bored, scared or hungry etc.

- Something about the physical welfare of the individual, for example, if they experienced any physical discomfort or symptoms i.e. headaches, nausea etc.
- Any thoughts, feelings or impressions that the individual have that they consider may be related or linked to any event or personal experience or to the location.
- The observed movements and actions of others within the group and those of occupants and visitors.
- The use of any equipment i.e. camera or thermometer – noting the reason for any picture or measurement.
- The time and duration of refreshment and toilet breaks or other periods away from the allocated area.

Sometimes, it may be the case that several people present are likely to have witnessed the same event. In these circumstances it is preferable that individual notes are written before any discussion or conversation regarding the event that has taken place. Any temptation to amend the notes in any way following discussion must be avoided.

Members of the investigation group should be encouraged to record in their notes their entire time at the location rather than only noting those events or experiences which they consider to be unusual or unexpected. Including items which at the time may not seem particularly relevant, such as the lights from passing vehicles or external sounds that have an obvious cause may be helpful in providing additional context to any experiences that are of interest.

Although some guidance may be desirable, with the exception of time and location information, in most instances the individuals should be given the freedom to decide what they consider to be noteworthy and what is not.

The coordinator should collect together all of the notes from the group. This may be done periodically throughout the investigation visit or it may be left until the visit is completed. Sometimes, individuals may offer to send their notes later or to re-write them in a more legible form. It is always preferable to obtain the original notes as there is a tendency for people to reconsider their notes and comments afterwards and to edit or amend them in some manner, perhaps after discussion with others who were also present. Issues of legibility etc. can be easily dealt with later by the reader contacting the writer.

Where the notes contain information that pertains to a person's state of mind, their physical condition or some other personal information, that information should normally remain confidential from other members of the group except in those circumstances when the person has given their permission for them to be made available.

At the end of each visit the coordinator must ensure that all remnants of the investigation visit have been removed and the location has been left in the same state and manner in which it was found.

12 | Research Resources

In addition to the information that may be obtained from talking to witnesses or from time spent at the location the investigator will frequently seek other sources of information in order to further their knowledge of the case. Sometimes, a great deal of information will be readily available including books and articles pertaining to the location may have been published. Sometimes, the location or its ghosts may already be well known locally through word of mouth and circulating gossip. In other instances, it may have already been investigated by other investigators and their accounts and reports published in some form. Each of these strands of information need to be examined by the investigator and added to the case file.

However, the investigator must be cautious. They should avoid placing any undue emphasis on any particular item of information and wherever possible try to trace the origin of each account and story. Often the investigator will find that newspapers and books simply repeat previous accounts verbatim, or at other times adding or changing some of the details. From time to time the investigator may encounter a witness who appears eager and willing to share their own strange experiences and theories about the case, but they may soon discover the account is either fictional, grossly exaggerated or a repetition of something previously heard. It is certainly not uncommon to find several variations of a ghostly encounter existing in the locale as a result and it is also not unknown for almost identical accounts of ghosts and hauntings to have been relocated from other locations nearby, or sometimes further afield.

12.1 *The historical perspective*

The belief that apparitions and related phenomena are connected with some past event or person is rooted deeply within our folklore and culture and conducting research or studying the history of a haunted location is commonly and routinely carried out by investigators.

Sometimes, investigators may undertake an investigation based entirely upon the recorded or reputed history of the site, or because of something significant that took place there or perhaps because someone significant is associated with it. Sometimes an investigation is undertaken simply because the location is old.

Researching the history of the location, the building and the people that have been associated with it may in some instances reveal information that is relevant to the investigation process. The investigator should be cautious that any knowledge gained or discoveries made whilst researching the history of a place or person does not result in the investigator merely trying to establish some link between the reported experiences and some event or person from the past. The investigator should be aware that the history or the appearance of a location may alter the perception of a witness and in some instances that of the investigator also. For example, a figure seen in a religious setting might easily be interpreted as being a monk or a priest whilst a similar experience taking place in a castle may become a warrior or a knight.

12.2 *Where to find information*

When it is considered to be useful to conduct historical research the investigator should use all of the available material, which could include regional and national archives together with local resources. In the first instance, many investigators will commence their search for information using the internet. This is a good starting point as an increasing number of archives and historical records are being placed online. But the investigator must be cautious whenever they are using online resources as some may contain erroneous information or may not provide any indication about the original source of the information.

Records that are provided by official organisations such as the National Archive, government and education agencies, are generally more reliable and many will often allow the investigator to download copies of the original documents for a fee. The Society for Psychical Research also has an extensive online catalogue of research pertaining to spontaneous phenomena and cases. Local and regional authorities are required by various acts of Parliament to maintain records and archives and to make them available for study by members of the public. These archives will often contain original documents and other material and it is common for many of the items to be unavailable or unsuitable for online inspection or reading.

These include land use and planning information that often have very detailed maps and plans attached. It is also likely that many of the photographs that are held are represented online in the form of low resolution copies. Church records are another potentially helpful source of information about local births, deaths and marriages which may be helpful – many of these are centrally held although an increasing number are available online. Nevertheless, many still remain within the diocese or in the respective parish or church. Police and civil defence records may provide information relating to crimes or major fires. Currently, only those records pertaining to a limited number of Police forces including the Metropolitan police are held in the National archives. Other force records are held in the regional and county archives. The majority of National and regional archives and records may be accessed freely, although there is often a fee payable for making copies of material.

Newspapers, including national, regional and some local editions usually have an archive of past issues which the investigator may find helpful. The larger newspapers may have their archives available online. When using newspaper archives, the investigator need to be aware that the newspaper may be more concerned about presenting a story to its readers rather than any concerns about complete accuracy of the content.

Privately managed local history websites may also be helpful and many include tales of ghosts and haunted places, but these sometimes contain erroneous information and occasionally present local folklore and legend as factual information.

The investigator should not confine themselves to only searching for information online. Local libraries can prove to be a useful resource and will normally contain books and newspaper clippings that are of local or regional interest. Some of the books and material may be available for loan, whilst other items may only be viewed in the reference section. Larger libraries may also hold detailed local maps and plans, collections of photographs of local interest and copies of local newspapers. Regional and local museums are also worth visiting and will often contain material within their collection that is not available elsewhere. In addition to the national and county museums there are many independent and specialist museums that cover almost every aspect of society and industry. In many towns and even small villages, there may be a local history society or group. These can be a valuable resource and it is common for information about locally known hauntings or other unusual experiences to be included. It is not always the case that these small societies or groups will have their archive or contact details available online, although information regarding these societies may be usually found by enquiring at a local library or information centre.

12.3 *Additional information resources*

Investigators may sometimes desire or require information about the geology of a location or weather information for some period in the past. There are several online resources such as the British Geological Survey and the Ordnance Survey who provide detailed information which is available to view and download, including maps of various scales and types, geological maps and information about seismic activity. There are a number of other online resources that also provide both recent and historical weather information. The investigator needs to be aware that whilst many internet weather data sites will allow the user to enter precise location coordinates the provider will normally use information from the nearest weather reporting station which may sometimes be tens of miles away from the actual location. Most sites will inform the user which weather reporting site the data was collected from but some do not, which could be misleading.

12.4 *Stating the source*

In most instances the investigator must record and state clearly within their report the source of any information that is accessed and used. This record should include the specific details of records and documents that have been used, the location of the particular record within an archive and the date upon which it was accessed. This allows others who wish to review the investigation to also examine the original information. In the case of internet searches it is also good practise to include the URL of the relevant page and the date upon which it was accessed.

The need for client or location anonymity may preclude some of the information from being made available publicly, but it would normally be included in the report that is made available to the client and other interested parties which the client has approved.

13 | Investigation Methods

Investigators of ghosts, hauntings and related phenomena have explored many methods in their search for evidence and to help them in investigating a case and bringing it to a conclusion. The evidence for ghosts etc. remains circumstantial and there are many opinions, ideas and beliefs of what these phenomena represent and how they manifest. As a result, some investigators use methodologies that follow established scientific principles whilst others favour techniques that are derived from psychic methods. The majority of investigators prefer to combine both scientific and psychic techniques in their investigations.

13.1 *Scientific methods*

Some investigators mistakenly consider that using scientific methods relate specifically to the use of equipment and technology. This is not true; in order established methodologies which science has evolved and that use a logical series of steps which are followed in order to produce a conclusion.

- Discovering the phenomena or experience. This may come by way of the testimony and accounts of others, or by observing or experiencing some phenomenon first hand.
- Hypothesising an explanation for the phenomenon or experience.
- Testing the hypothesis by experiment or observational study.
- Evaluating the results of the test. Subsequent to which, it may be necessary to then modify the hypothesis and carry out further tests and evaluations.
- Draw a conclusion based upon all of the evidence that has been gathered.

The scientific method considers all forms of information and evidence, including that which is gathered from witnesses, equipment and all other sources. It may be applied to any set of circumstances that the investigator might encounter.

13.2 *Psychic methods*

Psychic methods, including those derived from spiritualism such as mediumship, table tipping and the Ouija board rely almost entirely upon either human testament or human involvement in order to provide information. Where such methods are employed, it is necessary to fully document the testimony and account of all those who are directly involved. Some of these methods may produce physical effects, i.e. the table may move or tilt and the pointer may move to indicate a letter. It is important that the investigator seeks to distinguish between an actual physical effect and a reported or perceived effect. For example, it is not uncommon for people to report that they feel colder or warmer during séances and paranormal investigations, but it is much less common for temperature measurements to be made in order to try and corroborate these reports.

When conducting experiments that involve psychic methods the investigator needs to be aware that they may be dealing directly with an individual's deeply held beliefs and convictions and they must remain respectful and courteous, permitting the individual to adequately express their views. However, the investigator should avoid placing any emphasis on information derived by claimants of special abilities and also be aware it is often difficult or sometimes impossible to demonstrate that the information being provided is false. Regardless of whichever methods are used, the investigator should:

- Avoid any pre-determination regarding the nature of any phenomenon or possible cause based upon their own beliefs and desires or those of the client.
- Ensure that the appropriate controls are applied in all tests and experiments to avoid errors or the possibility of deliberate fraud occurring.
- Properly document and record all of the experiments, tests and information obtained in order to provide a comprehensive account of the entire investigation process.
- The account should also include the rationale i.e. the reasons and basis for each of the various experiments being conducted.
- Ensure that all of the information obtained using the various methods is fully considered. Evidence or testimony that does

not support the hypothesis or the desired outcome should not be dismissed or given reduced emphasis.

13.3 *Investigating large locations*

Often, the investigator will be faced with trying to investigate a location that has multiple rooms, sometimes spread over a number of floors or a large area. It is always better for investigators to concentrate their resources including team members, into areas where previous reports of experiences are known to have taken place but it may not always be clear beforehand which specific areas are of most interest. In these situations, most investigators will routinely adopt an approach of moving around the location, going from place to place or room to room periodically. Each is then inspected in turn before moving on to the next. At other times, the investigator may spread their resources throughout the location. These methods may be helpful if the number of site visits are limited but using either method makes it more likely that the investigator will miss a significant event, simply by being in the wrong place or having their resources too widely spread. However, in those cases where the investigator has the opportunity to make a number of visits then it is worthwhile considering dividing the location into a number of zones or areas.

The investigator is then able to concentrate their available resources into examining just one or two zones per visit, rather than the location as a whole. After several visits it may become apparent that some zones are more interesting; perhaps as a result of experiences or events that occurred during the investigation or perhaps because of unusual or unexpected recordings and measurements that were taken. These zones of interest can then be more intensively scrutinised during subsequent visits, paying much less attention to zones that had proved to be less interesting.

14 | Equipment

The majority of the evidence that relates to apparitions, poltergeists, ghosts and kindred phenomena comes in the form of witness testimony and subjective accounts of events or experiences. In these circumstances, the investigator is forced to rely upon the frailties of perception and memory. In order to have some additional means of obtaining information which may be helpful in understanding the phenomena, the investigator may wish to use various devices and items of equipment as part of the investigation process. Properly obtained measurements and recordings are not subject to any deficiencies in memory or perception and are free from any bias due to belief and desire. Often, the equipment used will take the form of cameras and audio recorders although many investigators also use additional instruments, either regularly or from time to time. Investigators now routinely measure temperature, electromagnetism and a range of other physical variables.

Used correctly, equipment may be able to:

- Verify that an observed phenomena or event actually occurred.
- Quantify the amount of change or the rate of change of an observed variable over time.
- Observe and record events that may go unnoticed by human observers.

Measurement data and recordings obtained by the use of equipment often constitutes a significant part of the overall evidence that will need to be considered.

Properly obtained measurements and recordings can provide information that may confirm or contradict the claims of witnesses. In addition, measurements and recordings may be helpful when testing some hypothesis or support a conclusion.

14.1 *Choosing and using equipment*

With regard to the selection of items of equipment for use during an investigation, the investigator must take notice of the fact that currently there is no device which has ever been demonstrated to have the capability to measure or record paranormal phenomena. Periodically, certain photographs and other measurements have proved difficult to satisfactorily explain but these do not constitute proof of the existence or otherwise of any supposed paranormal phenomena. Whenever the investigator decides to use any item of equipment it is important that steps are taken in order to ensure the quality and the reliability of the measurements and recordings. These include:

- Selecting the correct item of equipment for the particular variable that is to be observed or measured.
- The equipment must be used in accordance with the manufacturer's instructions for use.
- The equipment should be placed in a suitable position and in an appropriate manner.
- The operator should be familiar with setting up the equipment and ensure that it is operating correctly. Many devices provide a range of options and settings that need to be selected by the operator before use. With devices that are used less frequently, it is helpful to include a copy of the instruction manual with each device as a reference.
- The operator need to be aware of situations in which error or misuse may result in the measurements or recordings being erroneous. It is a common occurrence for investigators to walk around hand-holding devices that are designed to be used in a static situation.
- Information should be recorded in a way that it can be recalled and interpreted correctly. Some devices allow the measurements to be recorded automatically whilst others may require the measurements to be written down by an observer.
- The investigator must ensure that each device (or observer) is using a common system for recording the information. In situations where multiple devices are used for obtaining measurements of the same variable, they should be set-up to use the same measuring scale i.e. Fahrenheit or Celsius, milliGauss or microTesla.
- If the device has the provision to record the date and the time, the investigator needs to ensure this has been set correctly. It is important that this is checked prior to each use as it common for the clock to become less accurate over time or following a change in daylight saving. In some devices the date and time must be reset after each battery change. It is

helpful to have a master clock which all equipment and the participant's watches are set to at the commencement of the investigation visit.

• It is good practise to ensure that each device to be used is tested beforehand and in good working order. Should any device require calibration, this too should be carried out as specified by the equipment manufacturer.

The investigator must be aware of the manufacturer's stated accuracy of each device that they are using. For example, if two identical thermometers with a stated accuracy of +/− 2 degrees are being used for obtaining measurements in the same place and under the same conditions then it is acceptable for the two devices to display values which disagree by up to 4 degrees. However, both would be expected to show a similar amount and rate of change in response to any ambient changes. Thus, it is usually more helpful for the investigator to concentrate their attention upon the amount of temperature change or the rate of temperature change over time, rather than simply comparing the values that are displayed.

Irrespective of whichever variable that is being observed or measured there will often be a range of devices available to the investigator. These options include devices that are intended for domestic or consumer use and other devices which are intended for professional and commercial use. Those devices intended for professional use are generally more accurate, more reliable or have a greater degree of accuracy than their consumer orientated counterparts. However, this normally comes at an increased cost, which is often many times that of a consumer equivalent. Devices intended for professional use must adhere to one of the recognised series of standards which govern the accuracy and the operation of the equipment. However, due to the prohibitive cost of such devices, it is generally impractical and unrealistic for investigators to make measurements and observations in accordance with these devices, but it should nonetheless be the aim of the investigator to undertake all of their measurements and observations to the highest possible standards. Equipment should be selected which provides the greatest possible accuracy and reliability for each particular variable that is being measured and be used in accordance with the manufacturers instructions at all times. It is generally better to have one or two higher quality devices positioned in places of interest rather than a multitude of less capable devices distributed throughout the location.

14.2 *Equipment precautions*

The investigator needs to be extremely cautious of devices that purport to be able to capture evidence of paranormal activity. There is a growing range of devices and contraptions that are sold for use on paranormal investigations and the manufacturers make various claims regarding their capabilities. Specifications, where they are provided, are often vague or make claims that cannot be substantiated. Sometimes, it is unclear what the device is actually measuring and also the units of measurement that are used are not always specified. Controls for the various settings are frequently not properly labelled so that it is impossible to make any meaningful measurements with the device. Investigators should also be aware that it can be equally difficult to obtain any useable measurements from devices which are designed for simple operation. For example, some meters that indicate levels of electromagnetism do so only by means of an ascending series of coloured lights – green, yellow and red etc. Whilst this may be helpful when making a rapid assessment of overall levels i.e. higher or lower, the investigator is provided with very little information regarding the actual levels of any detected electromagnetic field.

The inappropriate use of equipment will result in measurements and recordings having no value to the investigation. In some situations, it may even result in the investigator becoming mislead by the information that is obtained. The investigator should avoid the selective use of any measurements and recordings. Information must not be discarded merely because it does not conform to an expected or hoped for outcome. It is important that all of the information that is obtained from the equipment is included and considered. The careful and well considered use of the appropriate equipment is more likely to produce measurements that are meaningful and which will withstand scrutiny.

14.3 *Baseline measurements*

Many investigators will routinely make a series of measurements before and/or during the investigation against which all subsequent measurements can be compared; such measurements are often referred to as 'baseline measurements'. It is not uncommon for these comparative measurements to have been obtained prior to the investigation or under different prevailing conditions which are different from those which existed during the actual investigation visit. Therefore, the investigator should expect that there will differences between the various sets of measurements. The investigator needs to exercise caution when using any comparative measurements, particularly when the prevailing conditions were very different. Measurements taken in the middle of night will be different from those taken during the day and measurements obtained in a busy location full of people will be different from those when just a few people are present. Seasonal variations and other external factors such as the weather or passing traffic will also cause differences in the measured values of many variables.

Measurement is the process of obtaining the magnitude or rate of change of a desired variable. By making measurements it is possible to determine if some part of the variable is abnormal or lies within a normally expected range.

The greatest degree of accuracy will almost always be gained by obtaining measurements over the longest period of time possible, as this will permit the highest number of samples to be obtained under the widest range of prevailing conditions. Measurements can also be used to determine additional information about the particular variable. For example, the maximum, minimum and average values and the rate of change over time.

The availability of data-logging technology now allows for a range of variables including temperature, humidity and electro-magnetism to be sampled and recorded automatically. Selecting high sample rates may be helpful in revealing transient events that have a short duration and which might otherwise be missed. Instantaneous measurements, i.e. those which are obtained over a very short period, are of limited value to the investigator. For example, briefly measuring the temperature following a report of someone feeling it has become cold will only provide an indication of the temperature at that moment but give no information about any temperature changes prior to, or following the measurement being taken. In some circumstances it may be helpful to also obtain a reference measurement. This is an additional series of simultaneous measurements made using a separate device. For example, a recording thermometer placed centrally within a room can be used to provide a reference point for any other temperature measurements made within that same room. Likewise, a continually running video camera can provide a visual reference against which all other video footage of the same area may be compared.

14.4 *Recording the measurements*

It is important that all of the information provided by the use of equipment is properly documented and that it can be correctly understood and interpreted afterwards.

Some devices have the ability to record the measurements themselves to some form of memory whilst others may rely upon them being read and the information noted down separately.

The investigator must ensure that a common standard is being used by all those who participate in the investigation for every variable that is being measured. For example, if measuring the temperature, it should be decided beforehand which scale, Celsius or Fahrenheit, is to be used. Without this, it becomes much more difficult to relate one series or set of measurements to another.

The precise placement of every device should be carefully noted, together with a note of which device (including the make and model) is being used at each particular location. Failing to adequately document not only the measurements themselves but also how and where they were obtained increases the likelihood of the resulting measurements being considered to be less reliable.

14.5 *Making excessive measurements*

Many investigators prefer to use every possible means of obtaining some type of evidence during their investigation visit by adopting a technique of measuring and observing everything all of the time. This may be tempting, but over-measuring can generate an inordinately large amount of data for the investigator to sort through and carries an increased potential for the investigator missing any significant data. Therefore, it may be more beneficial to consider the selective use of equipment, measuring or observing only those phenomena that have been reported or are of interest. For example, if nobody has ever reported an unexpected temperature change then measuring the temperature is unlikely to be helpful. Likewise, if temperature changes are a commonly reported occurrence but no apparitions or object movements have been reported, the use of a camera may not always be necessary.

14.6 *Completing the measurements and recordings*

Many investigation groups will have a shared pool of equipment, whilst others use a combination of group and personally owned equipment. The variety of equipment in use may result in several data and recording formats being used, both electronic (i.e. data-logging) and manual (notes and charts).

Upon completion of every site visit it is important that all of the data and the recordings from the equipment is collected together promptly.

Where a particular device uses a removable type of memory i.e. card or tape etc., it is a straightforward task to collect together the various recording media, retaining them at least until they have been examined. A suitable box or bag labelled and dated for each site visit is normally sufficient. Other devices may use a non-removable memory to store the data, these can normally be connected to a laptop computer and the information copied directly into a dedicated folder labelled with the location and date information. If time permits, this can be undertaken prior to leaving the location or as soon as is practical afterwards. It is good practise to retain the original recordings on the device until the copy has been checked to ensure that is has been correctly copied, since mistakes can sometimes occur when transferring data. Handwritten notes of measurements should be collected together, ensuring that all pages are numbered and labelled with the location and date together with a note of who recorded the measurements and the equipment that was used.

In the event of individuals within the group using personally owned devices during the investigation, a copy of all the information from the personal equipment should be obtained and added to the case file at the earliest opportunity. Wherever possible, this is done prior to leaving the site. Once an individual has left the site, taking their equipment and the recordings away with them and with the intention of sending the information in later, there is a risk that either the data or the recording may be changed or altered prior to it being received. Such changes do not necessarily indicate fraud – they may be unintentional and accidental as a result of a format change or data compression being applied during the transfer process. Only complete and unedited recordings and measurements are to be accepted and if possible, the original recordings or measurements retained until the copies have been checked as they may need to be referred to should any questions arise from the copied material. In most instances, it is helpful to have a nominated person carry out or oversee this task. They ought to be familiar with the various methods that may be required in order to copy or transfer the data or recordings.

15 | Following the Site Visit

The importance of collecting together all of the information that has been gathered during the visit has already been stated. This includes all of the personal notes or investigation diaries and the information from any devices that have been employed. The collected material must be properly labelled and added to the case file.

The investigator needs to ensure that whichever labelling system they employ; it shall include sufficient information to allow it to be correctly interpreted at a later date.

No information should be disregarded or deleted at this stage, even if it appears to contain nothing of any significance. It is not uncommon to find that additional information may be discovered days, weeks or even months later which may alter the significance of information obtained earlier.

It is perhaps a good idea to place the information obtained from the investigation visit to one side immediately afterwards, as often those involved will be tired and may not be in the best mental state to begin sifting through the information. There is almost never a requirement for the investigator to provide a conclusion or outcome immediately and to attempt to do so will only serve to increase the risk of mistakes being made due to tiredness or undue haste.

15.1 *A systematic approach*

The recordings and the notes should be examined systematically; this might for example be by location, i.e. room to room. In the case of audio or video recordings it is often better to have two people watching or listening to the recordings. To prevent fatigue, listening sessions should be restricted to around thirty minutes before a suitable break is taken, a minimum of fifteen minutes' break is suggested before resuming the task. If anything is seen or heard that may be of interest during playback, then a note should be made of whereabouts on the recording it is situated, together with a brief description of the type of event. At this stage it is better to complete the entire preview of the entire recording rather than focussing on any individual item, however interesting it may appear to be.

The personal notes and investigation diaries should also be read through systematically. Once again, it is better to read through the complete set of notes and diaries highlighting any items of interest in order to return to them later.

Once all of the recordings and notes have been examined, any items that have been marked or highlighted can be looked at again. Work through each item thoroughly, checking the recording or notes against all of the relevant supporting material. The investigator should compare the other notes and recordings made at the same time, paying particular attention to those which may offer some further insight into what might have transpired.

For example, if it is noted in an investigation diary that a particular person felt suddenly colder then it is worthwhile examining temperature data for the period of time immediately preceding and following the time of the reported experience. Likewise, if an unusual sound is recorded on one device, then it is worthwhile examining other audio recordings made around the same time. Often, the written notes or the video footage might also reveal something of interest, such as a team member or some other person connected with the visit moving around and being the unwitting cause of the sound.

The investigator must avoid the temptation to immediately judge that any event, however strange it may appear, represents something paranormal or anomalous. Neither should they presume that an event must have a natural cause if one is not immediately apparent. Each event of interest needs to be considered carefully and compared against the all of the available information. Information from witness testimony and the information that is gathered during visits to the location should be drawn together towards forming a hypothesis regarding what may have occurred.

15.2 *Search for patterns*

When developing a hypothesis, it may be helpful to examine the case file for any patterns or events or experiences that may be connected. For example, does the phenomenon occur at the same time or on a particular day? Is it only reported in a certain place or by a particular individual? This type of search may reveal significant information about the nature of the phenomenon.

It may also allow the investigator to target their resources over additional visits and look more closely at some particular place or at some particular time. For example, if a particular sound is heard or recorded at a given time then it may be worthwhile re-visiting the location at the same time to see if the same sound is repeated. However, it is sometimes the case that no pattern will be forthcoming or the event is unique or is so infrequently reported as to appear so. In such instances, the investigator can do little more than document the particular event or experience as completely as possible.

15.3 *Develop and test your hypothesis*

When all of the strands of information have been sifted and examined the investigator may attempt to form an opinion or develop a hypothesis regarding the phenomenon. A hypothesis should take the form of an idea or notion that can be tested to determine if it is viable and plausible. Testing the hypothesis may take the form of replicating or recreating the circumstances or conditions that existed when the original event or experience was reported.

To use the previous example of a sound that was heard at a particular time, it might be hypothesised that it is due to some mechanism within the building, perhaps a domestic appliance operating. Likely candidates for the sound can be closely observed to see if they are responsible. If that is the case, then the investigator may reasonably conclude that the cause of that particular phenomenon has been located. If the appliance is found not to be the cause, then the investigator may then eliminate that device from their list of possibilities and move on to examining other potential causes, testing each in turn. It may be that in some instances no cause can ever be found for the event or experience that has been reported or recorded. In such instances, the investigator must avoid speculation and limit themselves to fully documenting the particular event in the case file, including details of all the tests that have been conducted relating to the particular phenomenon. In this way the investigator can demonstrate that they have considered and examined those possibilities even though no determination about the cause could be reached.

Guidance Notes

Every individual event or phenomenon should be dealt with in this systematic manner with the details of the hypothesis, tests and the findings recorded into the case file.

16 | Reaching a Conclusion

When all of the various phenomena have been examined and tested it is time to draw the case towards a conclusion. It might well be the case that the investigator finds that they are able to provide a reasonable explanation or a probable cause for only some of the events or experiences that have been reported or observed, and that with other events or experiences no explanation has been forthcoming. Sometimes, the investigator is able to say with some degree of certainty that a phenomenon was the result of some natural process or a misperception by the witness. In other cases, it may be due to the malfunctioning or the mal-operation of some appliance or device, including those being used by the investigator. In rare instances, the phenomenon may turn out to be a prank or hoax.

In other instances, the investigator may be faced with a phenomena or series of events that defy all attempts to explain satisfactorily. In such cases, the investigator may be a tempted to give these a label or a suggestion of paranormality but to do so would be an error as it would lead to a conclusion that cannot be substantiated. Current knowledge prevents such an absolute conclusion from being reached and in reality perhaps the best any investigator can conclude is that those phenomena are unexplained.

It may also be the case that further information will come to light at a later date that sheds some further information on the events which will permit another conclusion to be reached. It might also be the case that some future advancement of knowledge, or in the methods and the equipment employed, will yield more information. In such cases, the investigator may do no more than to document their investigation and their findings, placing them onto the record for future reference by either themselves or other investigations.

16.1 *Producing a report*

The final step of any investigation is producing a report that brings together all of the information and the processes that have been carried out, together with the findings and any conclusions that have been reached, into a report describing the investigation. In some instances, this report may be for a client whilst in others it might only be for the investigator or their group's archive. Sometimes, the report may be shared publically or privately with other individuals or organisations. In some instances, it may be necessary or desirous to provide a report of the same case for both private and more general reading. The need to protect the anonymity and privacy of all parties has already been discussed. However, when producing a report intended only for the records (and the eyes) of the investigator or in those instances where the investigation has been commissioned by a client it is usually acceptable to include the proper names and full details of the location. In circumstances where the investigator has been instructed by those involved, such as a witness to omit some or all of their personal details, this information must be anonymised within the report.

In the event of a report that is intended to be shared more widely, a more stringent approach to protecting the identity of those involved must be employed. This policy must extend not only to names and personal information, but should also include removing or changing any references in the report that might provide unwitting clues about the location or the people involved. Particular attention should also be given to any photographs or supporting material that is included within the report. The investigator must ensure that written permission has been sought prior to using or including in the report any pictures, video or audio recordings that they may have made during the investigation. Sometimes, a client or location may wish to promote their particular case or location within the media or the social media themselves. In such instances, the investigator may decide if they are asked, to provide details of their involvement or provide a copy of their investigation report, but the investigator should be mindful and respectful of their ethical responsibilities towards all involved parties.

The investigator should normally refrain from approaching the media directly about a case or providing a copy of their report to any media organisation or representative. Such an approach may lead to unwanted attention and may cause distress or nuisance to witnesses or to the location. Investigators are advised to confine themselves only to the task of investigating the case and not to act as a publicity agent for the client or location.

Whatever format the investigator chooses to use, be it electronic, paper or some combination the report should commence with a brief summary of the case and any significant findings. The summary, together with the body of the report, needs to be written clearly and concisely using plain language and avoid the use of unnecessary jargon, acronyms or abbreviations. Descriptions of measurements made using any devices, should include some information about what the device is and what it was being used for. It may also be helpful to the reader to include some basic information about the rationale and reasons for selecting and using a particular device.

This is particularly the case with reports that are written for clients who may have little or no previous knowledge of ghost investigations or the terminology and expressions that are commonly used by those who carry out investigations. without including some definition or explanation. For example, the person reading the report may not know what is meant by the abbreviation 'EVP' and may never previously have heard of electronic voice phenomenon.

The report should concern itself with providing factual information relating to the case, i.e.

- Why was the investigation carried out?
- What was experienced? By whom, where and when?
- What did those who were questioned say in response to the questions they were asked?
- What were the results of any tests, measurements or experiments that were conducted?

The report should avoid introducing the personal beliefs of the investigator or include ideas that cannot be substantiated. The report must avoid using statements that appear to be definitive and which may be interpreted as representing a proven concept. For example, "ghosts are able to manipulate energy" or "spirits can communicate electronically using this device". In reality such statements are speculative and represent notions or ideas that are not proven.

In instances where the investigator has carried out any experiments as part of their investigation then the report should include information about why each experiment was carried out. This information needs to be presented in a form that the reader can find helpful and perhaps follow-up if they desire.

63

The report might usefully include links to research documents and other supporting information rather than relying on less helpful statements of reason such as, "some people believe that..." or "it is thought that...".

Witness interviews or their responses to questions may be included or discussed within the report. To aid the reader, the report may include partial sections from the complete interview in the body of the report. However, it is often helpful to also include a full transcript of the interview including the questions into an appendix or supplementary section so that the reader can refer to it if they wish. Likewise, the investigation diaries and notes of the investigators may be dealt with in this same manner.

It may be helpful to include plans of the location, showing the general layout of rooms and placement of witnesses or significant features. Plans should be labelled so that the location and placements may be readily understood. If it is decided to include photographs these too need to be labelled appropriately. Whenever plans or photographs are included then they must be linked to the relevant parts of the report.

The results of any measurements obtained should be fully considered within the report, not only those results which support the hypothesis that is being tested but also those which do not support the hypothesis. The investigator might consider including the complete set of measurement results in an appendix or supplementary section.

Whenever the investigator has accessed any records or archives this information should also be included within or attached to the report, noting the place the material was stored together with the relevant catalogue or filing references and when it was accessed by the investigator. This information too, may be placed into an appendix or supplementary section.

17 | Additional Resources for Investigators

These notes for the guidance of investigators of spontaneous cases are precisely as they are entitled: 'notes for guidance'. It is not intended that these should be the only source of information for investigators. The Society for Psychical Research, through it's website, has a series of supporting pages for these notes that provide investigators with up to date information, articles and helpful links. In addition to the SPR, there are a number of other organisations in the UK and also overseas which may prove helpful to the investigator.

17.1 *The Society for Psychical Research* – www.spr.ac.uk

The Society for Psychical Research was set up in London in 1882, the first scientific organisation ever to examine claims of psychic and paranormal phenomena. They hold no corporate view about their existence or meaning; rather, their purpose is to gather information and foster understanding through research and education.

The Society is a registered charity run by a council of elected members, with committees overseeing various activities. Past presidents have included philosophers, scientists and a British prime minister. Members from all over the world represent a variety of academic and professional interests. Members receive quarterly issues of the scientific *Journal of the Society for Psychical Research* together with the quarterly *Paranormal Review* which contains less formal articles on a variety of topical subjects. The Society welcomes all those who wish to learn about the subject. The Society holds an annual conference together with a series of talks and study days on a range of subjects.

17.2 *The Association for The Scientific Study of Anomalous Phenomenon (ASSAP)* – www.assap.ac.uk

ASSAP is a scientifically orientated educational and research charity dedicated to a better understanding of anomalous phenomena including ghosts, telepathy, mediumship, UFO's, Fortean phenomena and Earth mysteries. ASSAP was founded in 1981 and maintains close relations with many other anomaly and paranormal investigation groups including a national network of affiliated groups. ASSAP welcomes members with a broad range of paranormal interests. ASSAP holds an annual conference and hosts a series of investigator training days.

17.3 *The Ghost Club* – www.ghostclub.org.uk

The Ghost Club is the oldest organisation in the world associated with psychical research. It was founded in 1862. Past members have included Charles Dickens, Peter Cushing, Peter Underwood and Harry Price. The Ghost Club is a non-profit social club that offers open minded, curious individuals the opportunity to debate, explore and investigate unexplained phenomena. The Ghost Club holds monthly meetings and produces a quarterly journal, it also holds its own investigations and location visits.

17.4 *The Parapsychological Association* – www.parapsych.org

The PA is the international professional organisation of scientists and scholars who are engaged in the study of psi (or psychic) experiences such as telepathy, clairvoyance, psychokinesis, psychic healing and precognition. The PA was established in 1957 in Durham, North Carolina, USA at the proposal of Dr. J.B. Rhine. Emphasis was placed upon the professional character of the association and on promoting better communications between scientists working in the field. There are five levels of membership including 'supporting member' which is open to anyone. The PA hosts an annual convention and produces its own Journal and Bulletin.

17.5 *The Parapsychology Foundation* – www.parapsychology.org

The parapsychology foundation is a not-for-profit foundation which provides a worldwide forum supporting the scientific investigation of psychic phenomena. Incorporated in 1951, by the medium

Eileen J. Garrett, the foundation has remained committed to two goals: To support scientific and academic research into psychic phenomena; and to provide professional resources and information to the academic and lay communities. The foundation holds an annual Parapsychology Research and Education Free online course (ParaMOOC) and maintains an extensive library of works dedicated to psychical research.